BLACK BU$INE$$

African American Entrepreneurs & Their Amazing Success!

Black Jazz, Pizzazz & Razzmatazz™

by Carole Marsh

Editorial Assistant: Jenny Corsey • Graphic Design: Cecil Anderson • Layout: Lynette Rowe

Published by

GALLOPADE™
INTERNATIONAL

800-536-2GET
www.gallopade.com

Gallopade is proud to be a member of these educational organizations and associations:

The National School Supply and Equipment Association
The National Council for the Social Studies
Association for Supervision and Curriculum Development
Museum Store Association
Association of Partners for Public Lands

Black Jazz, Pizzazz, & Razzmatazz Books

Our Black Heritage Coloring Book

The Big Book of African American Activities

Black Heritage GameBook: Keep Score! Have Fun!
Find out how much you already know—and learn lots more!

Black Trivia: The African American Experience A-to-Z!

Celebrating Black Heritage:
20 Days of Activities, Reading, Recipes, Parties, Plays, and More!

Mini Timeline of Awesome African American Achievements and Events

"Let's Quilt Our African American Heritage & Stuff It Topographically!"

The Best Book of Black Biographies

The Color Purple & All That Jazz!: African American Achievements in the Arts

"Out of the Mouths of Slaves": African American Oral History

The Kitchen House: How Yesterday's Black Women Created Today's
Most Popular & Famous American Foods!

Other Carole Marsh Books

Meet Shirley Franklin: Mayor of Atlanta!

African American Readers—Many to choose from!

Table of Contents

A Word From the Author

Dear Readers,

Remember the last time you bought a comic book in a bookstore? Had your hair cut in a barbershop? Saw a movie in a theater? Then you have benefitted from the world of business!

America has a **capitalist** economy. That means that American citizens are free to operate their own businesses. The government cannot take control of a business, but *can* pass laws to ensure it operates ethically and morally. The government can also tax businesses (like citizens) to generate revenue that goes back into the community.

America is known as the land of opportunity partly because citizens are free to earn their living as they please. Every day, people start their own businesses, either alone, with a partner, or with a group of investors. A person who starts her or her own business is an **entrepreneur**.

African Americans have excelled in business and entrepreneurship across many fields of industry for decades. They have invented new products to meet needs, created businesses to provide important services, and worked hard to make their businesses succeed despite many obstacles. Some even become millionaires in the process!

Have you ever thought about starting your own business? It's not easy, but it can be fun, profitable, and educational! In this book, I have given you **20 Steps** towards the creation of your own business. You'll find helpful tips, fun facts, and encouraging stories of other African American business people along the way. I'll warn you now... it will be tough not to be inspired!

You'll probably be bursting with ideas after a few pages, but who wouldn't be? The possibilities are endless! Keep an "idea notebook" to jot down whatever spills out of your racing mind. Then you'll know what you want to achieve at the end of the book when I ask your creative side to take over! Lots of kids come up with great ideas that go really far, so let's start learning, and growing, and creating together!

Carole Marsh

STEP 1
THINK ABOUT IT!

Most entrepreneurs (of all ages) get their start by having an IDEA. A *new* idea. Even if it is a variation of an old idea, an entrepreneur still thinks his or her way to do or make something is newer, better, faster, cheaper, smarter, or even sillier!

Later, when the idea makes "the first million," and you see the idea or product, you might say, "Why didn't I think of that!"

So, THINK OF THAT!!! When you have a good idea (even if it's a little far-fetched, strange or different), write it down. Keep a little notebook of your ideas. One, or many, of them may be the tiny seed of a big business success!

THE GOLDEN TOUCH

Leonard Golden worked for a large company for many years and made a lot of money as a successful salesperson. But then he noticed that the company did not seem to think their employees had much value when they got older. He wondered what would happen to him when he got older! What would the company do with him?

Instead of waiting around to see what might happen, Golden made a very brave decision and thought of his very own golden idea. He decided to start his own sales company where he could work to the ripe old age of whenever!

Golden founded the ASAP Uniform Company, and became the president. Now his company sells many different kinds of uniforms, including hats and shoes. He calls business a game and says he likes to play! The playing wasn't always easy. Golden had to learn many new things, like computers and software, to make his new business grow. But Golden was willing to invest the time necessary to make his success happen!

STEP 2

PLANT THAT SEED!

When you really feel confident about that great and original idea, concentrate on it. Think about it. Think about it some more. Observe what other people have done with their ideas.

Now look at your idea from all angles. Will it keep until you are older, smarter, richer? Or is it something that needs to be done soon? Can you do it even if you are a kid? Or do you have to be an adult? How much space, time, money, machinery, and skill will it take to bring your idea to reality? Can you do it alone or will you need help? How much money will you need to produce your product or service?

Think about all these things *first*. The answers to these questions help make a good idea look better than ever... or make what looks like a good idea look like what it really is—not such a good idea. Better to find out now than later!

Wally "Famous" Amos thought his cookies would do better on the shelves than other brands, so he founded Famous Amos Chocolate Chip Cookies in 1975. His company earned $2 million during the first two years! He was the first black to open a cookie retail business!

Garrett Morgan came up with a new idea to protect people from toxic fumes. He created a gas mask in 1912. His idea won the grand prize at the Second International Exposition of Sanitation and Safety! His gas mask helped save many lives of construction workers, soldiers who fought in World War I.

Granville Woods created a railway telegraph in 1887. He made a business of selling inventions to the American Bell Telephone and General Electric. Woods sold more than 35 patented inventions!

STEP 3 — LEARN THE LANGUAGE!

If you ever decide to work in the world of business, you must learn to speak the language. There are words that sound hard (like "invoice") but are really just a business word for something very simple and ordinary (a "bill").

How can you learn to speak this language? Ask your parents or a business person, read a business book in the library, browse the Internet, or use your dictionary.

Every basic business word you learn will help you. You don't need to know them all (most adults don't even know all of them), but you should know a few! Check out the new words below!

expense: a purchase which costs a business money
Example: That new $3,000 printer was a big expense for us

income: money that a business earns
Example: Our last job brought home $50 income!

profit: money left over after all expenses are subtracted from the total income
Example: With those last few sales, we made $500 profit this month!

trend: a new shift or change in direction
Example: The newest fashion trends this winter seem to be leather boots, wool coats, and cashmere gloves.

competitor: another business that wants the same customers as your business wants
Example: We better increase our services to keep our best customers away from the competitors!

STEP 4 — COMMUNICATION IS KEY!

You need to learn to communicate if you want to work in business. Learn how to express your thoughts and ideas in plain English. Big words aren't always important. Sometimes "simple" works best!

First you need to know how to communicate **inside** the business. Learn how to write a one-page memo, a basic budget, and a plan about your idea or business. People won't ever agree with your ideas unless you can express them well. You also need to know how to give a presentation or deliver a speech about a business topic, research, or a new idea you want to share.

You should know how to communicate **outside** the business. The way you talk with customers is important for sales. People won't buy your new product if they don't trust you or think you aren't serious about business. Be polite and friendly! Know your product's strengths and be able to explain any weaknesses.

Lastly, you must communicate with the **media** about your business. Newspapers, magazines, television, and radio are all good ways to tell people about your product. You can write press releases (short articles) to send quick facts to reporters. Be prepared and know your business and products during interviews. News about your product will get out there!

LOOK HERE!

The first client that Terrie Williams signed up with her public relations firm in New York was Eddie Murphy!

In, 1853, the first black American woman to edit a newspaper, Mary Ann Shadd Cary, (1823-1893), began working for the *Provincial Freeman*, a paper devoted to the interests of black people in Canada. She actively encouraged other free blacks to seek refuge there after the passage of the Fugitive Slave Act in the United States.

STEP 5 USE YOUR BRAIN!

Think ahead. That's what entrepreneurs and inventors do every day. If something seems too hard, it just may be too hard. Think of an easier way. If it costs too much, think of many alternatives. Ask others for their opinions, ideas, or help.

Consider different solutions to the problems, and you may come up with even more ideas than when you started. All of this brainstorming will make your ideas better and better, and closer and closer to becoming real.

...ometimes problems lead to better ideas, ...solutions lead to nowhere. Don't be ...id to bend, twist, or reshape your ideas ...til they actually work.

Humpfrey H. Reynolds patented an improved window ventilator for railroad cars in 1883. The Pullman cars were used with his new invention, but no one paid Reynolds anything for his idea because he was black! He sued and won $10,000.

Lunsford Lane, a slave and a remarkable entrepreneur, earned the $1,000 price for his freedom by selling a homemade smoking tobacco mixture in several North Carolina cities like Raleigh, Fayetteville, Salisbury, and Chapel Hill. He eventually freed his wife and six children and moved North.

James Forten, Sr. invented a very creative sail-handling device. His windy idea was sold to many customers, and he made a lot of money. Forten later even owned a sail loft. In 1832, his company had 40 employees! Most importantly, Forten used his wealth wisely. His fortune enabled him to donate funds to the abolition movement and helped bring about the end of slavery.

BE CREATIVE!

STEP 6

Remember that an entrepreneur thinks of *new* things. Think of what services or products people need. What would make people's lives easier or better? What void can you fill in the marketplace?

You have to know what is going on in the world to do this. You have to listen. You have to think. Think big and think wild! When you have a good idea, you'll know it, and if it's really good then everyone else will too!

Some of the newest African American business successes by young people deal with history and culture. Popular sales items are sweatshirts with slogans such as "Know your history—Unlock your mind" (the United Negro College Fund slogan). Martin Luther King, Jr. tee shirts and African medallions are other examples of "Afrocentric" successes. What about kente cloth, khufi crowns dreadlock hair-dos, and special African ethnic clothin

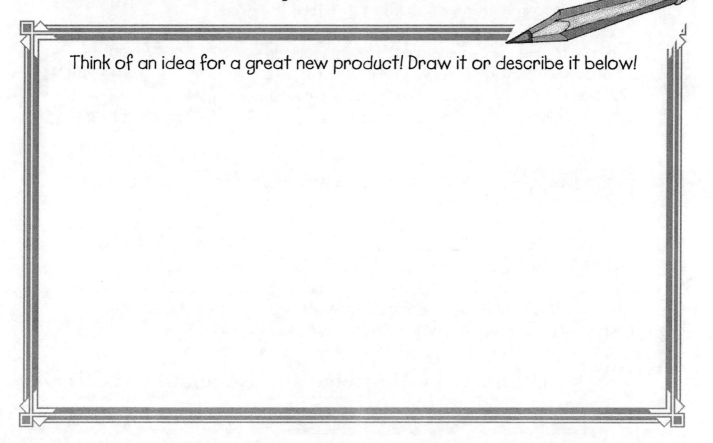

Think of an idea for a great new product! Draw it or describe it below!

STEP 7
THINK "FIRST CLASS"

$$$

Think of the good ideas that you have seen come to pass. Some of them only last a little while; some are around for a long time. So, no matter what your idea is, think of doing it the best you can. If it's pizza, let it be as good as Dominos! Think bigger; think better. Then you won't waste your time on an idea that might "take off" because it is clever, but might also "crash land" because it's cheap, sloppy, too slow, or doesn't taste good. Think smart **now** so your ideas will soar to success **later**!

MILLIONAIRE

MEN OF MANY FIRSTS

William Leidesdorff, (1810–1848), opened the **first** hotel in San Francisco in 1846, organized the city's **first** horse race, operated the **first** steamboat to sail on the San Francisco Bay in 1847, and became the **first** African American millionaire. In April 1848, he became chair of the California board of education, and was instrumental in opening California's **first** public school.

Reginald F. Lewis, (1942–1993), worked his way through college and attended Harvard Law School. He became a successful attorney and businessman by buying companies and selling them later at a higher price. He became the **first** African American to build a billion-dollar business empire when he won the auction of Beatrice Foods International in 1987. Lewis also made many contributions to education giving away millions of dollars to universities and other worthy causes. The Reginald F. Lewis Museum of Maryland African American History and Culture in Baltimore is named for him.

"Keep going, no matter what." —Reginald F. Lewis

HAVE A GOOD ATTITUDE!

STEP 8

Every entrepreneur has problems. There is just no way to create something new and not run into a million problems and obstacles that make it seem impossible to achieve your goal.

The "impossible" is what entrepreneurs are best at! When you have a problem, go back to your "ideas notebook" and think of another idea to get you around, over, or through it. Brainstorm, be creative, use your imagination, and you'll think of a solution, probably just in time for the next problem to arise!

Sarah Breedlove Williams Walker, later known as **Madame C.J. Walker**, (1867-1919), had to overcome some really hard problems before she became successful.

When her first husband was killed by some white men in Mississippi, she became a single mother of her young daughter Lelia. Walker moved her small family to St. Louis, Missouri, where her relatives could help her find work and raise Lelia.

After working as a laundress for a short time, she decided that she had to find another way to succeed in life. In 1905, Walker invented the "Walker Method" hair treatment to straighten kinky hair, and began to sell it. She soon married a newspaper man named C.J. Walker, but the marriage didn't last long. Walker suspected that her new husband was jealous of her business. His lack of support led to a divorce, and Walker was a single mother again.

But Walker kept going, and she eventually established a manufacturing company that employed 3,000 workers. In time, Walker became the first black female millionaire!

STEP 9 USE ALL YOUR RESOURCES!

You'll find that people like to talk to a person with a new idea. Sure, not everyone will think your ideas are as great as you do, but you can still use all your resources to get FREE help in developing your product or service to become successful.

Your librarian and the library are great resources! Parents and older brothers and sisters can be a big help. Teachers may also be willing to help you. What about a neighbor or friend? Someone who already works in a similar type of business (especially a small business) would be a great person with whom to discuss your idea.

Books, newspapers, and magazine articles are good information sources. Many industries have trade publications that you can read. Also, don't forget about the Internet, an amazing information source for all entrepreneurs!

The *National Negro Business League* was founded in Boston by **Booker T. Washington**. One of its charter members, **Eartha M. M. White**, (1876-1974), later became known as an "angel of mercy" in Jacksonville, Florida, for her work with the poor, financed partially by her many business ventures.

Multi-Cultural Publishers Exchange

The nation's first business incubator for small book publishers of color was located in Madison, Wisconsin. A business incubator is when a group of businesses join together to share office space, secretarial support, and other business services, like computers or shipping.

Small book publishers have grouped together like this so they can serve their customers better and give themselves a better chance to succeed by sharing resources and costs.

WRITE IT DOWN!

As you have problems, new ideas, and choices to make, write them down. You will find that what is written on paper is often easier to figure out in real life. Just by writing it down, even in a list form, you have helped your brain help you come up with an answer, maybe even a lot of answers!

What seems complex can often seem a lot simpler when it is written down. Then you can come up with various solutions and pick the best one. Maybe this solution won't come to you right away. But because you have written it down, you have given your brain something to think about while you are asleep. So don't be surprised to have an answer the next morning that you didn't think of before!

Berry O'Kelly (1860-1931) began a small business in the black community of Method, North Carolina (now part of Raleigh). His efforts on behalf of better agriculture, education, and industry led to a variety of tasks: chairman of a local school committee that consolidated three rural black schools into the Berry O'Kelly Training School; founder of the National Negro Business League; president of realty and shoe companies; chairman of a life insurance company; and vice-president of the Raleigh branch of the Mechanics and Farmers Bank of Durham.

O'Kelly explained how he managed. "My almost sole dependence now, when not conversing with deaf-mutes, is **pencil and pad**: they carried me through Shaw and Yale, and they have carried me through many important business deals. One can write with much more care and deliberation than he can speak. Did you ever think of it? A pencil puts one on his guard. Spoken words are easily forgotten, written words stay and are remembered."

MAKE DECISIONS!

STEP 11

Along the way to your new idea, you will have to make a lot of decisions. The odds are they will not always be right. That's okay because no entrepreneur (or anyone else!) is always right.

But no decision = no progress. So think, brainstorm, use your resources, figure it out, and make the best decision. You can always change your mind later!

FAST FACT: In 1893, the North Carolina Mutual Life Insurance Company became the first business owned solely by African Americans to secure $100 million in assets!

1963   James Phillip McQuay was the first African American to work in wholesale-retail fur manufacturing; he even won several design awards for his fur creations!

1970   Barbara Proctor founded Proctor and Gardner Advertising, Inc. in Chicago, Illinois.

1976   Union leader Addie L. Wyatt was the first black woman labor executive; she served on the Amalgamated Meat Cutters and Butcher Workmen board.

1990   Bertram Lee was the first African American to serve on the board of directors at Reebok International.

2000   Talk show host Oprah Winfrey launched her new "O" magazine, the latest in a series of highly successful business ventures including Harpo Productions, Inc. and television shows, "The Oprah Winfrey Show" and "Oprah After the Show."

STEP 12 TAKE RESPONSIBILITY!

Kids make great entrepreneurs because they are so creative and aren't afraid of new ideas. But it's not right to use your "just a kid" status as an excuse for not taking responsibility for the decisions you make. Everybody makes choices!

Take complete responsibility for your idea, for the facts you use to make your decisions, for your choices, for your service, for your products, for your successes, and especially for your mistakes.

These aspects are all part of being an entrepreneur, who must learn to have a good attitude and say:

USE THESE!

1 "Thank you very much!"
1 "Oops, I goofed."
1 "I'm sorry."
1 "Yes, I'll replace it."

One rainy night in the early 1850s, an African slave named **Stephen** fell asleep while watching tobacco cure over a wood fire. The fire nearly went out while he slept. When Stephen awoke, he quickly scrambled for something to rekindle the flame. Suddenly he turned to the pit where he had made charcoal for the forge. There he found several charred logs, which he placed directly under the tobacco.

Stephen later recalled, "To tell the truth about it, 'twas a accident." His accident accomplished what 250 years of experiments in curing and soils had not. The drying heat from the charcoal produced the unique flavor of what came to be known as bright-leaf tobacco.

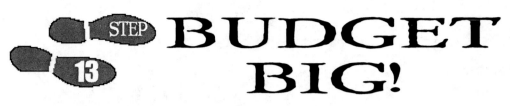

STEP 13 BUDGET BIG!

New ideas cost money. There is no sense kidding yourself about this. It won't help to guess, think, or hope that money will be there when you need it. All along the way, think about money, use your resources, figure it out, make decisions.

Perhaps someone will be willing to invest in your idea. You may have some savings you want to invest. You might borrow money. If so, be prepared to repay it whether your idea works out or not!

Know what your idea will cost so you can know what to charge for your service or product. Don't charge too much *or* too little.

Think about costs like advertising, materials, delivery, mistakes, returning someone's investment, interest on borrowing, etc.

You may need to "crunch some numbers" to answer these questions. Visit a bank or credit union, and interview someone to learn more about small business finance.

In 1903, **Maggie Lena Walker** (1867-1934) established the St. Luke Penny Savings Bank as a result of her work with a black fraternal organization to which she devoted most of her life. Maggie was the first black female to head a bank! Today this bank, known as the Consolidated Bank and Trust, has a net worth of about $37 million!

FAST FACT: In 2002, Serena Williams was the highest paid female tennis player in the world with earnings of approximately $4 million.

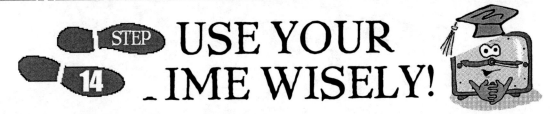

STEP 14: USE YOUR TIME WISELY!

An entrepreneur's greatest resource is time. If you are still in school, you will have to set aside some time to work on your idea, provide your service, or produce and sell your product. You can't shirk your schoolwork or chores, of course! Use every bit of spare time that you have: riding home on the school bus, waiting at the doctor's office, or sitting in the car on a road trip.

Plan your day and your time wisely. Schedule your day to avoid wasting time. You may be surprised about how much time you have and how much time you haven't used wisely!

African American Businesspersons Who Didn't Waste Their Time!

1885   D. Watson Onley built the first steam saw and planing mill owned and operated by blacks. The mill was built in Jacksonville, Florida. He also attended Howard University School of Dentistry to become a dentist!

1888   Fanny Jackson Coppins founded the Institute for Colored Youth in Philadelphia, which trained black youngsters in many different occupations.

1959   Ruth J. Bowen was the first black woman to establish a successful talent booking agency in New York City. She booked stars like Dinah Washington, Ray Charles, Aretha Franklin, and Sammy Davis, Jr. She started with only $500, but her great business idea became the largest agency owned by blacks in the world - in just 10 years time!

STEP 15 SET GOALS!

It's tough to know where you will be in five years if you don't know where you WANT to be in five years, 10 years, or 20 years. High school graduation? Broadway? College graduation? The NBA? Outer space? You don't have to know exactly, just start thinking and dreaming now!

Goals are a big part of that process, especially in busin Your goals should be timely and specific. For example, "I to read this entire book by Friday." Without being timely specific, it's pretty easy to skimp on your goals.

In business, goals are really important. You should have a schedule for when you want to start your service or produce your first product.

You should also set financial goals. How much money do you want to make, what are your costs, and what will you do with the money left over? You could reinvest it in your company or repay your investors. Which goals are the the wisest? Also you need a *contingency plan* in case things are late or you run out of money!

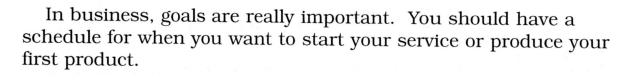

Ebony, Jet, and Negro Digest

John H. Johnson set some goals early in life. He was once a penniless child in Mississippi, but he worked hard at his goals. In 1942, he founded Johnson Publishing Company with a $500 loan, which he secured by using his mother's furniture as collateral. His efforts resulted in a successful business in Chicago.

Johnson's company publishes *Ebony, Jet,* and *Negro Digest* magazines. Today, he is also one of the richest black men in America!

STEP 16
PLAN FOR SUCCESS!

Smart entrepreneurs know that more businesses fail than succeed, especially small businesses. The down side is that these people often plan so much to avoid problems (like running out of money), that they forget to plan for success! That's setting yourself up for failure!

What if you sell twice as many products than you expected? Are your machines equipped to handle that much output? Plan for success! Can your employees provide that much service by themselves, or will you need some more help? Plan for success! Do your employees have enough time to produce, enter, ship, and bill all those orders? Plan for success!

Remember that you will face many obstacles in your path if you decide to start a business. People won't always agree with you, your family might not help, and the bank might not give you a loan. To battle these odds... PLAN FOR OBSTACLES TOO!!!

BLACK WOMEN WHO PLANNED FOR OBSTACLES

1905   Lucy Parsons (1853-1942) addresses the founding convention of the Industrial Workers of the World (IWW). This forceful speaker and activist in the radical Chicago labor movement was dedicated to organizing the working class.

1934   Dora Jones leads the first successful attempt to unionize domestic workers in New York City.

1937   The International Brotherhood of Sleeping Car Porters and Maids signs the first major contract between a black union and a large corporation, the Pullman Company.

1943   Moranda Smith (1915-1950) organizes tobacco workers in North Carolina.

STEP 17 TOOLS OF THE TRADE!

Starting a business takes time, and it takes tools! You should have everything you need to do a good job from the very beginning. Find a place to work, but get your parents' permission first before you take over the living room (and the kitchen, the dining room...)!

Set a time each day to work on developing your ideas and coming up with new ones. Find the space to design, tools to build, light to see correctly, and materials like paper and pencils.

Next to the ideas, your biggest tool should be the necessary funds. Without money, your ideas can't turn into products or services. You don't need a whole lot to get started, but you need something!

Start with the directions, the rules, the recipes—or whatever you need to do it right and on time. Set up a system and improve it as you go along. Remember that your ideas, your creativity, and your imagination are the most important tools in your tool box!

TOOLS OF THE TRADE

1 Education
1 Capital (money, funds)
1 Patience
1 Quiet place to work and think
1 Creativity
1 "Good Ideas" Notebook
1 Office supplies (paper, pens, calculator)
1 Confidence!
1 Support from family and friends!

1 Computer
1 Stamps
1 Telephone
1 Library nearby
1 Imagination

STEP 18 WATCH THE DETAILS!

Pay attention to details. If your new business is a paper route, don't throw the paper *near* the box or porch. Get it in or on it (each and every time), or you might find your "best entrepreneur friend" has just started the "In the Box" Newspaper Delivery Service!

Details are important because they can set you apart from your competitors in a good way or in a bad way. Like many other business aspects, details can make or break your sales potential.

For example, your lemonade stand serves lemonade with ice cubes made of water. Your neighbor's stand sells lemonade with ice cubes made of lemonade so the drink won't ever get watery, but will still stay cool. Which drink would you buy?

Details, Details, Details!

Nancy Green was born a poor slave in Montgomery County, Kentucky. She became one of the world's first African American corporate models.

The first instant pancake flour was introduced in St. Joseph, Missouri in 1889. The owners of the product wanted a unique way to market it. They hired Nancy Green to become "Aunt Jemima" and introduced her at the World's Columbian Exposition in Chicago in 1893. Nancy Green was 59 old! She served pancakes and charmed the omers with her friendly, down-home style. The cake booth drew such a crowd that policemen had ep in to keep people moving! Nancy was signed to a time contract and became a "living trademark" for Aunt Jemima Pancake Mix!

STEP 19 BE PROFESSIONAL!

"Yes, sir" and "No, ma'am"...
"We appreciate your time, sir."
"Please" and "Thank you for your business"

These words go a long way toward establishing a good reputation and good will with your customers and in the community. Does it really matter that much? You bet! So much so that businesses even assign a dollar value to the "goodwill" their company enjoys. Remember that folks remember your every word!

WAYS TO BE PROFESSIONAL

1 Be on TIME!!!!!

1 Have a firm handshake.

1 Make eye contact.

1 Dress professionally for every occasion.

1 Listen first, then respond.

1 Be prepared for any meeting; do your homework.

1 Think before you speak... how will your words sound to others?

1 Be courteous and respectful.

1 Don't chew gum or talk with your mouth full!

$$ Step By Step, To the Top! $$

Myrtle S. Potter began her career as a sales-person for a drug company. She worked long hard hours and gradually moved her way up the ladder. During the 1990s, she helped two companies work together to successfully sell a drug called Prilosec that helps treat heartburn. Today, Potter is the Chief Operating Officer of another company called Genentech. In 2003, Potter sold some of her stock in Genentech for $22 million!

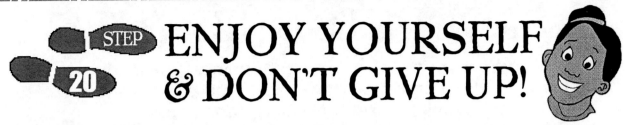

STEP 20 — ENJOY YOURSELF & DON'T GIVE UP!

One of the best reasons to work for yourself is to enjoy what you do. There's no sense in going to all this work to start a new business if you don't enjoy doing it. That's the great part about starting your own business. It's yours! You make the rules, set your own hours, and call the shots. And it's up to you to keep going even if you fail a few times, or even a hundred t   .

If your idea doesn't work, don't give up. Try again, or try something new. You'll find most entrepreneurs (who do all the things on this list) eventually end up with a successful idea. In fact, they often end up with *many* successful ideas!

In 1856, **Biddy Mason** (1818-1891) won her freedom in the courts of California. She worked hard as a midwife and nurse in the Los Angeles area. Biddy used her earnings to buy and sell land around the city to make a profit. She was the first black woman to own property in Los Angeles. Her careful investments led to a huge fortune.

Biddy never forgot where she came from before she   vealthy. In 1872, she provided a building for the   st African Methodist Episcopal Church in Los Angeles. She also opened the first daycare   nursery for local children who were homeless.

Devoted to charity work and aid to prisoners, Mason often said, "If you hold your hand closed, nothing good can come in. The   en hand is blessed, for it gives in abundance,   receives."

SUCCESS! SUCCESS! SUCCESS!

PRODUCTS & SERVICES!

Once you've come up with your great business idea, you need to figure out whether it will be a product or a service. You can start a business based on either type. People pay for both of these things, but they are different from each other. Products and services help meet different needs for the buying public.

WORDS TO KNOW:

PRODUCT: a useful and valued good produced for public demand
Example: baseball or refrigerator

SERVICE: useful labor that does not produce something tangible
Example: computer programming or auto repair

**Determine whether each picture is a PRODUCT or a SERVICE.
Check the correct answer box.**

1.
☐ product
☐ service

4.
☐ product
☐ service

2.
☐ product
☐ service

5.
☐ product
☐ service

3.
☐ product
☐ service

6.
☐ product
☐ service

Answers: 1. product; 2. service; 3. service; 4. product; 5. product; 6. service

CREATING A SERVICE BUSINESS!

Services provide people with a better, easier, or faster way to do things—and usually all three! Most folks don't have the equipment or skills necessary to do everything they want done. So they hire professionals to do the job!

For example, your dad might know how to change the oil in his car, but does he know how to install a brake system? He might need the services of a mechanic. But, if your dad IS a mechanic, then he might not! A professionally trained stylist can cut hair, but probably needs the postal system to send mail.

May I help you?

The circle keeps going because people have needs and other people are ready to meet those needs with specific service businesses.

SERVICE BUSINESSES

dry clean clothes	clean teeth	wax and wash cars
design websites	send mail	mow lawns
cut and style hair	polish nails	clean houses
walk dogs	invest money	baby-sit child

Design your own service business! Answer the questions.

1. What need does your service meet? Are there many people who will use your service? _____
   _____

2. What should people pay for your service? _____
   _____

3. Can you improve on an existing service? _____
   _____

4. What tools will you need to provide your service? _____
   _____

LET'S CREATE A NEW PRODUCT!

Time to pull out that "idea notebook" that you've been writing in while reading through this book! Pick your favorite idea. Now you can REFINE your idea, or make it better... to best!

Answer the questions to turn your great idea into a great new product!

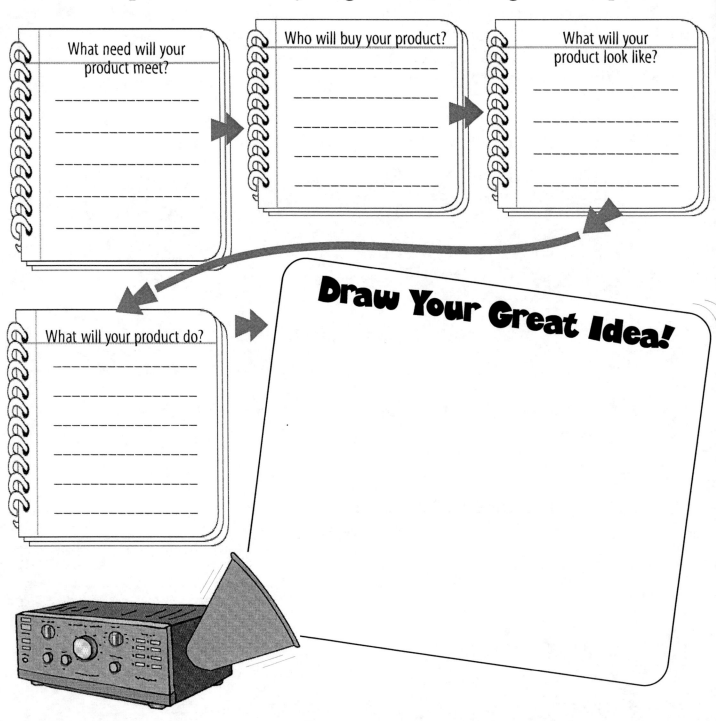

What need will your product meet?

_____

_____

_____

_____

Who will buy your product?

_____

_____

_____

_____

What will your product look like?

_____

_____

_____

_____

What will your product do?

_____

_____

_____

_____

Draw Your Great Idea!

LET'S SELL A NEW PRODUCT!

Okay, here's where your product can really shine or really sink. Even if you have a great new product, how will people know about it? What will you charge? How will you sell it? How you make any money?!?

Answer the questions below to sell your great new product!

PRODUCTION:
How will you make your product?

_____

_____

_____

ADVERTISING:
How will people find out about your product?

_____

_____

_____

PUBLIC RELATIONS:
How will stores find out about your product?

_____

_____

_____

PERSONNEL:
Who will you hire to help make, sell, and ship your product?

_____

_____

_____

FINANCE:
What will your product cost to make? How much will you charge for your product? What will your profit be?

_____

_____

_____

_____

EDUCATION GETS YOU THERE!

As you can see by now, "business" can mean many things: banking, retail, sports, art, music, manufacturing, publishing, transportation, services, education, acting, producing, dancing, insurance, and almost anything else you can think of that could bring in a profit.

Have you ever thought about starting your own business? There are many advantages to that type of career, but it's pretty easy to find some disadvantages as well. You are your own boss, but you have to pay your own paycheck too!

There are lots of kinds of careers and all kinds of ways to make money. The key to them all is education, of course! Education can make or break your career. Sure some people make it big without a degree, but what happens if things change? What about an NBA star who drops out of college to "go pro" and then injures his knee?

Education gets you there, but a lack of education can keep you right where you are. Do you want to move forward, get smarter, get successful, get there? Get educated!

African American Heroes in Education...

1870 Richard Theodore Greener, first black to graduate from Harvard University
1881 Booker T. Washington leads Tuskegee Institute
1888 Fanny Jackson Coppins starts school for blacks.
1904 Mary McLeod Bethune founds black college.
1907 Alain Leroy Locke, first black Rhodes Scholar
1921 Eva Beatrice Dykes, first African American woman to finish Ph.D. requirements
1924 Gwendolyn Brooks publishes her first poems in the *Chicago Defender* at age seven.
1960 Six-year-old Ruby Bridges is the first black child to desegregate a white school.

CREATE YOUR OWN IDEAS!

Draw a picture of your great business idea in each of the three boxes. These ideas can be products or services. Then name and describe your idea in the space provided. Be sure to say how your product or service will help people.

Idea #1:_____

_____

_____

_____

Idea #2:_____

_____

_____

_____

Idea #3:_____

_____

_____

_____

GLOSSARY

brainstorm: a process of thinking up ideas

budget: a plan for how to use your money

business: an organization that exists to sell products or services for profit

business incubator: several businesses that share common needs and expenses

capital: money

capitalist economy: allowing citizens to freely govern their own resources

competitor: businesses who work for the same customers in the same market

contingency plan: idea of what to do in case of emergency or problems

customer: buyer, consumer, or the public

education: entrepreneur's key to success

entrepreneur: a brave person who starts his or her own business with a great idea

expense: a purchase which costs money

generate: to bring in or create income

income: money that a business earns

invest: to put money in a business venture

labor: work done for pay

labor unions: groups that work to protect the rights and interests of employees

manufacture: to produce something

media: television, newspapers, radio

memo: short letter of communication

obstacle: problem to overcome

press release: short news article to media

product: a tangible item sold for profit

professional: responsible business person

profit: money left after expenses are paid

reputation: how the public thinks of you

resource: raw materials or people

revenue: income generated by a business

sales potential: possible income

service: useful labor

trademark: business symbol

trend: new shift in popular buying opinion

venture: an attempt to start a business

INDEX